María Daisy Quintana

Young Aunt Daisy about 1948. Picture shared by Desirae K, granddaughter of Aunt Daisy.

By
Stanley A. Lucero

María Daisy Quintana

By Stanley A. Lucero

Based on interviews by Raymond Kelso of María Daisy Quintana in 2005 and 2011.

Copyright © 2024

Stanley A. Lucero

ISBN # 979-8-89324-288-1

26963 Merril Avenue

Madera, California 93638

lucerito.net/genealogy.html

stanley.lucero@gmail.com

Funded by Pleistocene Foundation

Raymond Kelso, Owner

2362 Lumill Street

Ridgecrest, California 93555

Young Aunt Daisy in 1948 and older Aunt Daisy about 1996. Young picture courtesy Aunt Daisy's granddaughter Desirae K. Older Daisy picture taken by Yolanda Lucero.

Parents of Aunt Daisy: Manuel de Atocha Quintana and María Guadalupe "Lupita" Martínez. Picture given to my by Aunt Daisy.

María Daisy Quintana

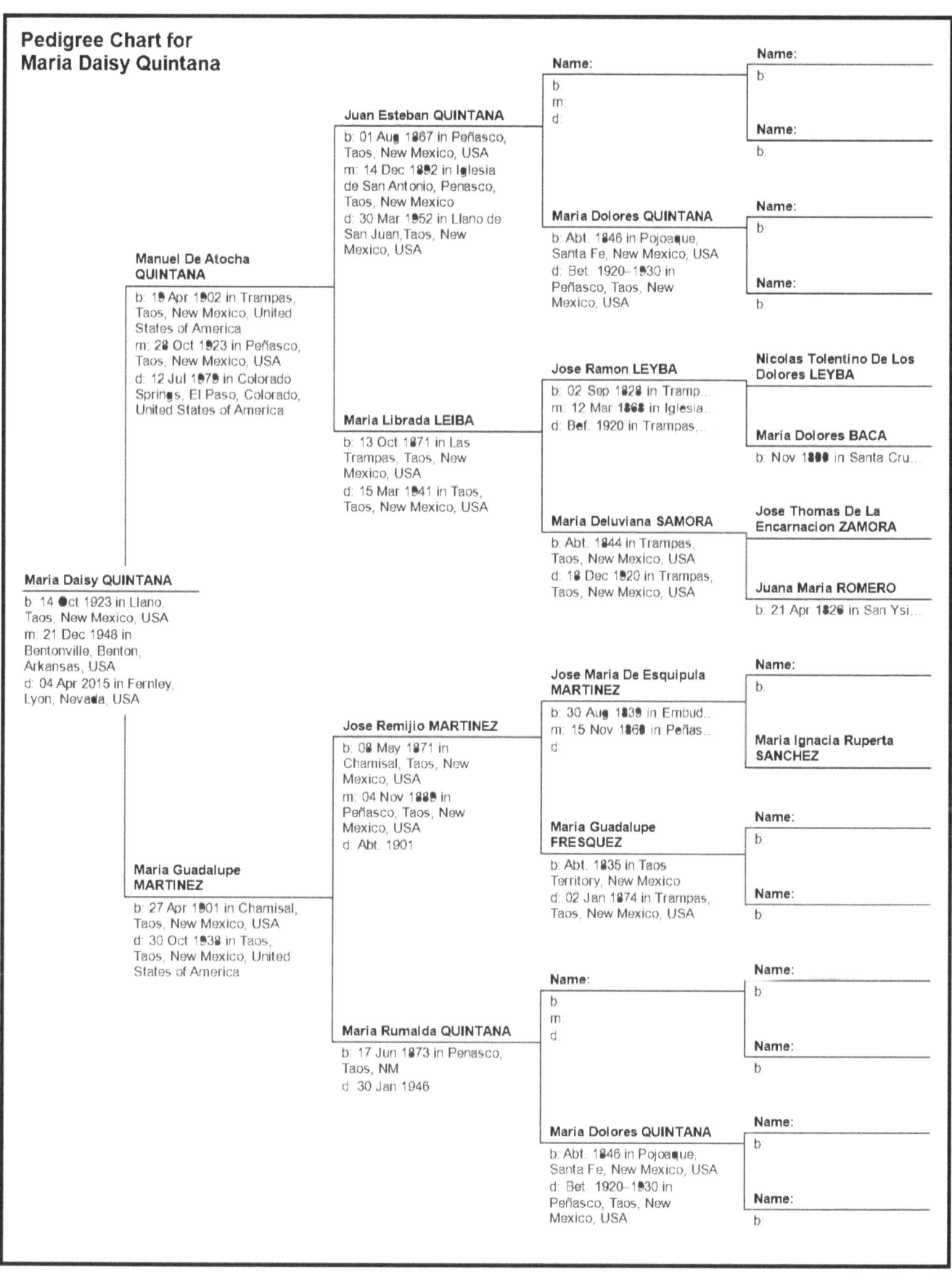

Daisy > parents > grandparents > great grandparents > great great grandparents.

Daisy was the Granddaughter of Juan Esteban Quintana and María Librada Leiba who were her paternal grandparents. Her maternal grandparents were José Remijio Martínez and María Rumalda Quintana. She was the great granddaughter of María Dolores Quintana who was the mother of Juan Esteban Quintana and María Rumalda Quintana [grandfathers unknown].

Daisy married Ernest Clay Shields on December 21, 1948 in Benton, Arkansas, USA. They had 3 children, Clarence, Patty and Ernie.

Her nephews Raymond Kelso, son of her oldest sister Lucille and Stanley Lucero, son of her younger sister Nadine have compiled a series of transcripts from interviews conducted by Raymond to tell her story. They have come together to share her story with the world and its readers within the pages of this book.

Raymond's and Stanley's Aunt Daisy passed away on April 4, 2015 in Fernley, Lyons, Nevada, USA and was buried next to her husband Ernest in Fernley, Lyons, Nevada, USA at the military cemetery.

Family Group Sheet for Manuel de Atocha Quintana and María Guadalupe Martínez
(Aunt Daisy's parents & her siblings)

Manuel 1902-1979 was the son of Juan Esteban Quintana 1867-1952 and María Librada Leiba 1871-1941.

Lupita 1901-1938 was the daughter of José Remijio Martiíez 1871-1901 and María Rumalda Quintana 1873-1946.

Manuel and Lupita were the grandchildren of María Dolores Quintana 1846-ca. 1922 from different unknown grandfathers.

Children of Manuel and Lupita from oldest to youngest.

- *María Lucila "Lucille" was born November 8, 1922 in Salida, Colorado and died November 1, 1996 in Ridgecrest, California. Lucille and Arl Ramond Kelso had two sons: Raymond Kelso and David Kelso. Lucille later married Jim Knights. They had one son together named Michael Knights.*

- *María Daisy was born October 14, 1923 in Llano, New Mexico and died April 4, 2015 in Fernley, Nevada. Daisy and husband Ernest Clay "Casey" "Shaky" Shields had three children: Clarence Shields, Patty Shields and Ernie Shields.*

- *José Nelson was born November 24, 1925 in Llano, New Mexico and died September 12, 1988 in Española, New Mexico. Nelson and wife Emilia Rodriguez had the following children: George Quintana, Joanna Quintana, Leroy Quintana, María Eden Quintana, Marie Quintana, David Quintana, and Gloria Quintana.*

- *María Amelia was born October 2, 1927 in Llano, New Mexico and died May 20, 1928 in Llano, New Mexico.*

- *Elizabeth Bessie Viola was born May 3, 1929 Llano, New Mexico and died June 23, 1930 in Llano, New Mexico.*

- *María Lourdes "Nadine" was born October 23, 1930 in Llano, New Mexico and died August 18, 2008 in Albuquerque, New Mexico. Nadine and husband Juan Amadeo "Mo" Lucero had three sons: Stanley Lucero, Bert Lucero and Noel Lucero. Nadine later married Tommy Smithson. They did not have any children.*

- *José "Benito" was born August 15, 1933 in Llano, New Mexico and died December 24, 1977 in Albuquerque, New Mexico. Benito and wife María Evelyn Erminia Frésquez had the following children: Wanda Quintana, Ben Jr. Quintana, John Quintana, Cheyenne Quintana, Victoria Quintana, Chuey Quintana, Lupita Quintana, Viola Quintana and Rocky Quintana.*

- *Antonio "Tony" was born March 28, 1935 in Llano, New Mexico and died October 27, 2003 in Colorado Springs, Colorado.*

- *María Virginia was born May 4, 1937 in Llano, New Mexico and died December 21, 1937 in Llano, New Mexico.*

- *Franklin was born October 29, 1938 in Llano, New Mexico and died October 29, 1938 in Llano, New Mexico.*

About Raymond Kelso

Arl Raymond Kelso Jr is the son of María Lucia (Lucille) Quintana and Arl Raymond Kelso Sr. This story is about María Daisy Quintana who was Raymond's aunt. Daisy's older sister Lucille and her partner Arl R Kelso had two children, Raymond and David. Lucille later married Jim Knights and had one son together. His name was Michael. He was Raymond's half-brother.

Raymond lives with his partner Dianne Foucher in Ridgecrest, California. Raymond and his former wife, Kathleen Clark had two daughters, Rachel and Sierra.

Living near his Aunt Daisy for many years, Raymond came up with an idea in 2005 to conduct a series of interviews with her to learn more about the stories of her life and the lives of her family while she was still living. He recorded these interviews to capture her "voice". As you read, you will hear Aunt Daisy's voice exactly as she spoke based on these recordings. No editing of how she spoke was done in this book to memorialize her true way of speaking.

About Stanley A. Lucero

Stanley Andres Lucero is the son of María Lourdes (Nadine) Quintana and Juan Amadeo (Mo) Lucero. The true storyteller in this narrative, María Daisy Quintana, is Stanley's aunt. Stanley is the son of Daisy's younger sister Nadine and her husband Mo. They had three children, Stanley, Bert and Noel.

Stanley Lucero is the author of this book. He lives with his wife Yolanda Lucero in Madera, California. They have five children, Mariano (Mario), Nora, Juan Miguel, Pedro Antonio and Nicosol (Nicky).

Stanley, Raymond's cousin, is a retired educator and an avid genealogist. Raymond and Stanley often talked about their family's history and their ancestors based on the records and details that Stanley uncovered in his family history searches. After Raymond conducted the interview with their Aunt Daisy, he decided to entrust Stanley with the transcripts to be converted into this book. These transcripts, along with Stanley's records have been compiled to create this story. Together, they hope that a small piece of their family's history will be remembered through the pages of this book for generations to come.

The home of my sister Nadine in Stringtown, Colorado: brother Tony, daughter Patty, nephew Stanley, son Clarence, sister Nadine, nephew Bert, and dog Spot. 1952. Picture taken by Aunt Daisy.

Author and Nephew Stanley, Aunt Daisy, and her son Clarence about 1996. Picture taken by Yolanda Lucero.

Aunt Daisy's Dad Manuel, nephew Stanley, and daughter Patty in Stringtown, Colorado, 1951. Picture taken by Aunt Daisy.

Aunt Daisy's Nephews Raymond and Stanley on Rio Grande Gorge Bridge north of Taos. Picture taken by Raymond Kelso.

Stanley A. Lucero

Comments By Stanley

"My first cousin, Raymond Kelso, son of Arl R. Kelso and María Lucila [Lucille] Quintana, interviewed our Aunt Daisy on two separate occasions. He recorded the interviews on cassette tape and then arranged for a friend to transcribe the cassette tapes. He sent the two transcriptions to me and asked me to turn them into a book. I kept the words of Raymond and Aunt Daisy exactly as spoken so that we could hear their voices. I added as many pictures as possible of the people and places mentioned during the interviews. Most of the pictures were given to me by Aunt Daisy.

Our grandparents, Manuel Atocha Quintana and María Guadalupe "Lupita" Quintana were married in 1923 at the Iglesia Católica de San Antonio in Peñasco, Taos County, New Mexico, USA. Grandpa Manuel was born in Trampas, and Grandma Lupita was born in Chamisal. They had ten children: María Lucia [Raymond's Mom], María Daisy, José Nelson, María Amelia, Elizabeth Bessie, María Lourdes [my Mom Nadine], José Benito, Antonio, María Virginia and Franklin. They only spoke northern New Mexico Spanish and learned English later in life.

They lived on the east side of Llano next to the "acequia madre" [mother ditch] on about 30 acres of land with a bird's eye view of Peñasco and Rodarte.

Our ancestors were a part of the 1751 Trampas Land Grant and the 1796 Santa Barbara Land Grant. Most of the land is now designated as the "Kit Carson National Forest."

With the loss of the land grants, our relatives were forced to leave their ancestral lands in search of work to support their families, pay for property taxes, and pay for the federal government fees to use the resources of the Kit Carson National Forest [grazing, fishing, hunting, firewood collection, "vigas" for houses and corrals, etc.].

My grandfather picked crops in southern Colorado and ended up working as a sheepherder in Wyoming during the summers. In 1938, while Grandpa was working in Wyoming, our Grandmother Lupita died in childbirth along with her newborn son Franklin. By the time Grandpa came home, some of his children were being raised by our relatives. My Aunt Daisy was living with her paternal grandparents and my Uncle Nelson was living with a Quintana aunt and uncle. Sometime later, my mom was sent to live with relatives in Leadville, Colorado.

When my Grandfather Manuel died in 1979, a man named Demetrio Ortega came to the funeral at the cemetery and introduced himself as a son of Manuel de Atocha Quintana. It appears my grandfather had relations with a woman named Gabriela in Peñasco between 1939-1950. They had three boys: Demetrio, Henry and one more boy who died without a name. My half-uncle Demetrio invited us to a reception at his home in Peñasco. I learned that only my Mother Nadine already knew about her half-brothers. The rest of the family at the funeral did not know about them. I don't think my Aunt Daisy ever learned about this family because she did not mention Demetrio or Henry during the interviews.

After my Grandma Lupita died my Grandpa Manuel married a young girl named Emilia Valdez. Emilia was younger than his two oldest daughters, Lucille and Daisy. Grandpa and Emilia's children were, Estela, Macario, Leroy, Guillermo, Agustin, Steve, Bessie, Patricia, Esedor, and Leroy.

Aunt Daisy married Ernest Clay Shields [also known as "Shaky" and "Casey"] in 1948 in Benton, Arkansas. They had three children: Patty, Clarence, and Ernie.

María Daisy Quintana

Aunt Daisy lived in New Mexico [Llano, Alamogordo, and Santa Fe], Colorado [Leadville and Aurora], California [San José, Milpitas, Lancaster, China Lake, and Ridgecrest] and Nevada [Fernley and Carson City]. Most of her jobs involved making beds at hospitals, hotels, and motels.

Her first language was Spanish, and she moved into the all-English world when she married Uncle Casey. Uncle Casey loaded torpedoes in a submarine in the Navy, worked on several Naval Bases, and purchased a TV repair shop. They had the first color TV in Carson City. Uncle Casey and Clarence also had a bar in Carson City.

I was privileged to meet my Aunt Daisy only a few times in my life and wish we had been closer."

Interview Transcript
First recording made in the Spring and Summer of 2005.

RAYMOND: "Who are the children in the family?"

DAISY: "Lucille María born on November 8, 1922, in Aleda [Salida], Colorado. Daisy María born October 18, 1923, in Llano, New Mexico. Nelson in Llano, New Mexico. Nadine (Lourdes) María in Llano, New México. Amilia [Amelia] in Llano, New México. Died as a baby of measles or chickenpox. Can hardly remember her. Betsy [Bessie] in Llano, New Mexico. Died young. Benito José in Llano, New Mexico. Antonio in Llano, New Mexico. Two more kids, Virginia, died, and then a boy [Franklin]. Mom died in childbirth."

DAISY: "There were no shots available. A lot of kids died of measles or chickenpox at that time. Father and Mother were first cousins. They eloped to Colorado. Father was 18, and Mother was 20 when they married. His name, Manuel Atocha Quintana. Hers, Lupita María Martínez. After Lucille was born, [they] got married in Llano. It costs $25 to get married. Father had to borrow $5 to come up with the money. The Priest wanted $25. They didn't have the money, so he lowered the price to $5. They were probably married at the church, although you could get married anywhere, like in your yard. Mother is buried in the church graveyard in Llano. Father in family cemetery, Quintana Cemetery, donated land. Most people were Catholic, baptized as babies. The way Catholics hold the people, get money."

Juan Esteban Quintana. Aunt Daisy's grandfather, born in Llano, son of María Dolores Quintana, half-brother of Rumalda, and father of Manuel Atocha Quintana. Picture shared by Dallas [Quintana] Eggelmeyer.

Grandma Lupita and baby son Franklin are buried inside the wood-framed fence in the middle of the picture to the left of the Llano Catholic Church. Picture taken by Raymond Kelso.

Grandpa Manuel is buried in the Quintana Cemetery in Llano near "el cuchillo" [the knife].
Picture taken by Raymond Kelso.

Acequia Madre In Llano

DAISY: "Llano is smaller now. Now they've got electricity, water. When I lived there, they got water from the ditch right by the door in bucketfuls."

RAYMOND: "Were the floors dirt?"

DAISY: "The floors in the house were wood. "Seca Madre" ["acequia madre"], the mother ditch where he built the cabin out of wood logs. There was a root cellar ["soterrano"] half underground. He got logs from the mountain. Filled mud and straw between the logs."

NOTE: The "acequia madre" was dug from the upper Santa Barbara canyon at the foot of the "La Jicarita" peak to bring water to the Llano area. It is along the east side of Llano, overlooking Rodarte, Peñasco, and Rio Lucio. Llano is at 8,054 feet above sea level and about 300 feet higher than Peñasco. Aunt Daisy lived by the "acequia madre" looking down at Rodarte.. [Stanley]

RAYMOND: "Outhouse?"

DAISY: "Ya, outhouse ["común"]. Used kerosene lanterns ["lamparitas"]. Kerosene bought at the store. My first memories are "Cadito" ["La Jicarita" Peak], the huge mountain, bald at the top, you could see."

"La Jicarita" [elevation 12,808 feet] as seen from upper Llano.
Picture taken by Raymond Kelso.

RAYMOND: "Above the timberline?"

DAISY: "Ya. Everything green from March to June. It rained. Snowed in the winter. Prayed for the limited weather in the summer to get the wheat and corn."

RAYMOND: "How many brothers did your father have?"

DAISY: "Steven, oldest, my dad, María Romasita, Ramona. Big family of five. I knew three and two dead. All from Llano area down in the valley."

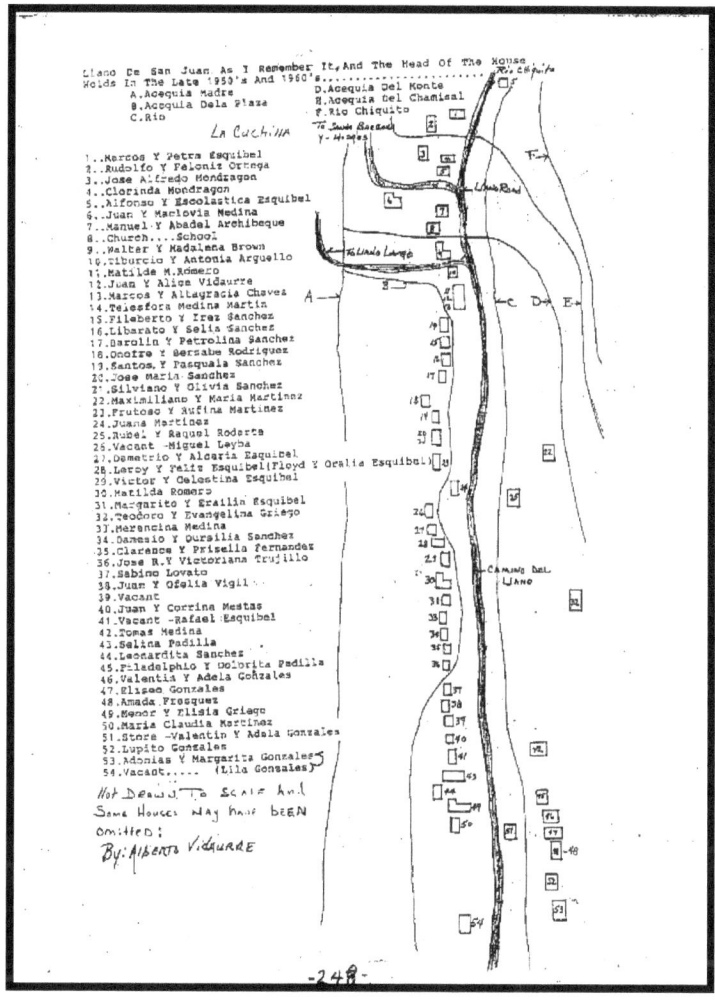

Map of Llano about 1950. Page 248 of Alberto Vidaurre's book, La Gente del Llano Nepomuceno. La "acequia madre" is labeled "A" on the left side of the map. The land of Grandpa and Grandma is to the left of the "acequia madre." It is approximately to the extreme left of the words "Camino del Llano." Unfortunately, Vidaurre did not interview the families that lived in this area. [Stanley]

DAISY: "Had a lot of property, 30 acres. We all lived on it. I remember playing with siblings. [she laughs] We worked. My Dad and Mom played baseball by the ditch in an open field. Planted alfalfa later. Me and Nelson played, well, rocks. We pretended they were cars, and we made a lot of roads. We had lots of chickens, few goats, took the goats to the mountains, six cows, a few milk cows, pigs. The pigs were fenced, and cows where there was grass. Our land [is] connected to Steven's land. At night, we brought the animals into the corrals. We had a lot of hay. I don't know where we got it. We planted wheat, peas, and corn. Farmed. Had carrots, cabbage in the garden. Some of the corn was for the pigs. Sugar, we had to buy but most of the goods come from their land. Mom took the wheat to the mill and got flour and the rest ground for the pigs. Potatoes had to be bought. We lived on potatoes and beans. The meat. We preserved it ourselves. Made tortillas. Had a cow shared with relatives. Neighbors got together. Cut into thin strips and lot of salt prevented flies and dried the meat. Like jerky. We had it with beans, hominy. They cooked great with the meat. We cooked with it. We couldn't eat it alone; it was jerky. We made most of our food

Sugar was purchased; maybe the lard came from the pigs. My grandmother made her own soap. They cooked part of the pig plus lye. Boiled it. It made soap to wash floor and clothes. Some of the clothes were made by Mom. She made her own. Later, she ordered out of Sears catalog. Mom died when a boy was born. I was 14. Lucille complained about Dad being away from home. There was no work. He had to go to Colorado or Wyoming for shepherding. Before Mom died, he had to go away for work. The men had to leave the house as sheepherders. Go to Wyoming with those big farmers. Two Uncles were sheepherders. After Lucille was born, they stayed in Colorado to work in the mines. Some of the time, he went by himself. Mom didn't work, too busy with kids. There was no birth control and Catholic."

RAYMOND: "Go to school?"

DAISY: "Grade school in Llano. A two-room schoolhouse, 1st grade to 4th. Peñasco High School a big building three miles away. That's why I quit, too far to walk. No road. Five or six kids walked together. Lucille quit at sixth grade. When Mom died, Lucille was 15 years old in the 6th grade. I was 14 when Mom died. When I went to high school, I was 18. I stayed in the 9th grade for three years."

Beronís Roybal and Alfonso Ortiz. Beronis was Aunt Daisy's first cousin. Picture shared by María Armijo Rodríguez. Aunt Daisy probably had to repeat 9th grade due to being a native Spanish-speaking student whose English skills were below grade level. The land for Peñasco High School was donated by Alfonso and Beronís Ortiz. Beronís was the daughter of María Antonia Quintana and Francisco Roibal and granddaughter of María Dolores Quintana. Alfonso is the forest firefighter who rescued the bear cub you know as Smokey the Bear. He would go to Apache Canyon by Chamisal every year to participate in Apache ceremonies.

After Mom Died

DAISY: "[My sister] Lucille was my Mom. Raised the kids after Mom died. Lucille and I fought because Lucille wanted to boss her [me] around. I didn't do anything. I was dumb. I helped Lucille with the cooking and washing clothes. She was the mother. Lucille did all the housework. She was around all the time."

RAYMOND: "Did Lucille have a boyfriend?"

DAISY: "She had lots of boyfriends. Just acquaintances. We knew everybody. This guy was working. He came home, and his sister was [a] friend of Lucille's. She kind of went to [with] the moment. There's no attraction. From uptown, boys formed little gangs. Happened by the store where the Catholic Church is. Lower Llano group and the Catholic Church group would fight like now. They didn't get together. Lucille was [a] friend with this boy and his sister."

DAISY: "Didn't go out on dates. Hung out together. In the wintertime, we didn't go out."

RAYMOND: "Was there a movie house?"

DAISY: "Nothing. Only the holy rollers [religious group] came to town. They were like entertainment to us."

RAYMOND: "Radio?"

DAISY: "When my dad went to Wyoming for 6 to 8 months with a 1934 truck and a radio in a suitcase. He stayed a month or two and left again. We played the radio 'til midnight."

RAYMOND: "Did he send money home?"

DAISY: "He left credit in the store. Couldn't buy nothing but food."

RAYMOND: "No candy or nothing?"

DAISY: "Oh, ya, candy. When I went to high school, no breakfast, just a piece of tortilla or a few beans, and I went to the store and got me a couple of candy bars. That's all I had all day. Walk home was 3 miles. I was never fat. Lucille was fat. I walked, not alone. Other kids walked with me. I did everything on my own. We didn't complain. We didn't know anything."

RAYMOND: "Did you ever go on vacation?"

DAISY: "No."

RAYMOND: "Picnics? Visit relatives?"

DAISY: "No. The first time to Taos, only 24 miles, it was after Mom died. Dad take [took] us to the city in the pickup. I thought we were going to eat in a restaurant. No. We ate by the river. Ranch meat and bread. I didn't want a picnic. I wanted a restaurant. We rode in the back of the pickup. I was 18 or 19. It was after Mom died. We went in the same pickup every summer to Colorado, Alamosa, La Jara to pick peas ["alberjones"]. We stayed and picked potatoes. When winter came on, we came home."

RAYMOND: "Where did you stay?"

DAISY: "They furnished the tent and outhouses. It was during the war. They need workers."

Step-Mother Emilia Valdez

RAYMOND: "Kids?"

DAISY: "My dad had a lot of kids, and then he married his wife, Emilia Valdez and took his [her] relatives, and we got in his pickup and slept in tents every summer."

DAISY: "Lucille was the first to leave. She left for Colorado, and we were in Colorado. She went to Red Cliff [a mining town at the foot of Battle Mountain] and Dilmon [Gillman, a mining town]. She knew someone there. She took the bus and left. Then Nelson left. In the meantime, Nelson got married. Him and his wife left. So, I was left with my dad and Emilia. He was already married, of course. My dad stayed with us five years. In the meantime, we all went and picked peas and potatoes for the last ten years. As far as I know, Emilia was there too. My stepmother. That's our life. We didn't have any entertainment."

RAYMOND: "Lucille said she got real angry [with her Stepmom] and didn't want to put up with Emilia."

DAISY: "Ya. I think she was jealous because my dad gave her all the authority. I don't know. I could get along with Emilia. Nobody else could. I don't know. Lucille couldn't get along with anybody. Sometimes. I don't know. Lucille, we couldn't get along together. Probably, she was an alcoholic then. I don't know. I can't remember. I didn't see her drinking."

1965 Quintana Family. Left to right sister Lucille Dad Manuel, Stepmother Emilia and Aunt Daisy. Picture given to me by Aunt Daisy.

RAYMOND: "I didn't see her drink a lot."

DAISY: "She was a diabetic too. You know. Diabetics are moody. My husband is moody. That's it, Raymond, no entertainment. In winter, we had entertainment 'cause it was Christmas. We had programs in the Presbyterian Church. In school, we had programs, but in the summer times, we just worked."

RAYMOND: "You were around when Emilia having kids. I suppose while you were still there?"

DAISY: "Ya. The one that died, [Stella] the oldest, was a year and a half the last time I was around Emilia."

Colorado And California

DAISY: "In Leadville, no kids, and Lucille was there too. She was at the cafe washing dishes. I worked at Pedom Hotel [Vendome Hotel, Leadville, Colorado] making beds. After Lucille left, I was in and out of Llano, Raymond. I went to Santa Fe and, worked for the hospital, and stayed there one year. Army hospital, soldiers. Soldiers that come sick from overseas. I was there a year. I rented a house with another girl, of course. Washed dishes around there, too, before that in Santa Fe. I was in and out of Llano then. I couldn't find a job after I quit the hospital. I stayed for a while. Oh Ya, I worked at the hospital in Santa Fe for a long time, another year. See, I wasn't home with Emilia too much."

1886 Tabor Grand Hotel, also known as the Vendome Hotel. Picture taken from a webpage for the Tabor Grand Hotel.

RAYMOND: "How old were you?"

DAISY: "Already 20 years old. I worked at the smelter [in Stringtown]. I stayed home like in Colorado. I worked a year there in Leadville. I was working graveyard. I walked. They had the power hammers, and I had to turn the key on for the hammers. That was my job. When the metal got stuck on those [power hammers], I had to turn it off. I had to turn the key on and let the metal [cool] down. I work a year there. That's when Lucille came over, and you was a baby. Father left, and Emilia didn't want to, so she stay there. Emilia moved to town someplace. So me and Nadine [Daisy's sister] lived there in that house. All had a job so I could wrangle. It only $6."

RAYMOND: "So that's when Lucille come to see us?"

DAISY: "You was a tiny baby, maybe only 6 months. I couldn't get over it. You was bald-headed. I never seen a baby bald-headed, and you were white, white."

RAYMOND: "Well, you ought to see my grandson, he's dark, dark."

DAISY: "And lots of hair?"

RAYMOND: "Ya, lots of hair, lots of black hair."

DAISY: "That's what I was used to. The babies at home, and here come this baby. Lucille with a bald-headed baby. You were good-looking then, not ugly, but bald-headed. I couldn't, no hair at all. Okay, she stayed only couple days. I think she come on the train to Johannesburg. I think she was coming from Seattle."

RAYMOND: "Ya, probably."

DAISY: "Me and Lucille were great friends, you know. She was my mother. She was my friend. She was my sister, and I missed her when she died. Just like Tony. I missed him, but I missed Lucille more. She was everything to me. She the only relative I had. My Mom was dead. Well, anyway, that's enough."

RAYMOND: "Well, I miss her too."

DAISY: "Well, she was an alcoholic, but that didn't bother me at all. Just if you'd interfere with her alcohol, she'd get mad, and I don't know why I did anything. Should have left her alone, but it didn't bother me. She, when she had alcohol, she was da, da, da. She was jolly and everything. At China Lake, remember?"

RAYMOND: "Oh, Ya, I remember."

DAISY: "What else do you want to know? No entertainment in Llano. No policeman. No jail. No bars. No drinking bars. None. There was one in Peñasco, but that was three miles away. We went to dances in Peñasco. Lucille and I. We walked. After Lucille left, I walked with my boyfriend. My relatives. My boyfriend came. Picked me up with his sister, and then we walked. That's the entertainment then. We walked home. We were dumb. Just for a stupid dance, we walked three miles."

Life In Llano

RAYMOND: "I assume it was beans and tortillas when you were in Llano?"

DAISY: "That's what everybody thinks. That's what they think the Mexican eats: tortillas and beans. Well, it is true because beans, especially and tortillas, but we had potatoes all the time. Mostly potatoes."

RAYMOND: "Potatoes didn't grow up there, did they?"

DAISY: "No, we bought them at the store. They bring them from Colorado."

RAYMOND: "You had to buy flour, all that stuff?"

DAISY: "No, when my mother died, we had to buy everything. But, before my mother died, we had wheat. She made the flour at the pueblo."

RAYMOND: "You were saying that when your mother was alive, you didn't buy much food?"

DAISY: "When my mother was alive, she did all the farming. They planted wheat and then took the wheat to a person. They produced flour with it."

RAYMOND: "You didn't make enough flour to ah."

DAISY: "No, we didn't but half of it we did."

RAYMOND: "About half?"

DAISY: "Ya, we did, and we had corn and meat, jerky. Meat and we cooked it with beans, oatmeal. Plenty to eat. When my mother was still alive. When my mother died, we bought everything. We go to the store."

RAYMOND: "So nobody knew how to farm?"

DAISY: "No. Everybody grows everything in Llano. Everybody."

RAYMOND: "Why didn't you guys take over where your Mom left off?"

DAISY: "Who? Lucille was only 15."

RAYMOND: "Okay."

DAISY: "Kids don't do that. My dad went to get some money in Colorado or Yuma, and they come back. Got money, and then he went again. But he took us every summer to pick peas [and] potatoes. So we had enough money then."

Step Mother Emilia Valdez

RAYMOND: "Do you pretty much go to the same place to work?"

DAISY: "Alamosa, La Jara, Colorado, which is nearby farm country. We stayed there all summer picking peas. Then we come home. In the meantime, my father got married and stayed five years. I was 14, 15, 16, 17, 18, 19. By the time he got married, I was 19, but I was still living at home with my dad. I still went to pick potatoes with Emilia. And Lucille went to Colorado. She left, and so did Nelson. Then, after that, when she started having kids, she have to. She moved to Colorado. They move to Leadville."

RAYMOND: "This was Emilia, you mean?"

DAISY: "Ya, the whole family."

RAYMOND: "And Emilia was how much younger than you?"

DAISY: "She was. I was 19 at the time. Not married. She was about 17, 18. I don't know, Raymond."

RAYMOND: "Where did your dad meet her?"

DAISY: "They all went picking peas and potatoes. Family."

RAYMOND: "He met her in Llano?"

DAISY: "No. Met her! Everybody knows everybody. Since she was a little girl. When my mother died. See, her mother used to visit my mother. Well, a bunch of kids. That's include Emilia. But, ah, we went to pick the things. That's where they start fooling around. Went to Alamosa for peas and potatoes. In the tent. We lived in the same tent. They started fooling around."

RAYMOND: "By tents, it sounds like real big tents?"

DAISY: "Ya. I remember we went to Alamosa, to town, and they left Lucille and me someplace, and Lucille was smarter than I was, and she said, "I know what they're doing." I said, "What are they?" "Renting a room." See, he was fooling around with her before she got married. I was dumb. I didn't understand those things, or I didn't want to. I don't know. I played with dolls with Nadine, and I'm 7 years older than her. I was. She was 7, and I was about 15,16,18. I still played with dolls with her. I didn't want boys. I was kind of funny. I didn't want boyfriends. It took me a long time. I never did like them to begin with. I don't think. [laughs] I didn't like [Cascy?] six years when I met him. I think I really wanted a home or something. No, I never wanted to get married. I remember that, and the reason is, I know that as soon as they got married, they started having kids. I want none of that. I don't want no kids. These Mexicans have a lot of kinds kids."

NOTE: When people ask me where I am from I answer New Mexico. They always ask me what part of Mexico I am from. I tell them that I am not a Mexican because my family has been in New Mexico before Mexico became a country. New Mexico was originally called El Reyno de Nuevo Mexico de Nueva Espana.

Religion

Old Mormon Church in Llano. The Quintana Cemetery is close to the church. Picture found on a report from the Church of Jesus Christ of Latter Day Saints.

Estevan and Bersabe Quintana donated the land for the Mormon Church in Llano. Estevan was my Aunt Daisy's first cousin. My Uncle Nelson was living with them in 1940. Estevan and Bersabe were baptized in the Church of Jesus Christ of Latter-Day Saints. Grandpa Manuel later became a baptized member but didn't go to church. Uncle Nelson and his family were also baptized members and left the church. Bersabe is the sister to my dad's mom.

RAYMOND: "Were you Catholic? Did you guys go to church on Sundays and that kind of thing?"

DAISY: 'No, we had no church. My dad sent us to the Mormon meetings in Llano for a while because they don't drink. They don't smoke and do bad things. So he push us to go Sunday with the Mormons. He cooked dinner for us once in a while. He didn't go to church, no church."

RAYMOND: "But basically, your mother had a little farm there?"

DAISY: "Thirty acres. We were little compared to the big farms in Colorado. They didn't grow enough, but everybody know everybody in Llano. So, like apricots, I don't remember where we got them. We used to dry them or dry them on canvas, and my Mom put a little veil over them for the flies, and they dried the apricots and we had them for, like candy. We had them. We peeled them and dried them out. My Mom was a worker."

RAYMOND: "Did your dad always take off in the summertime? As long as you can remember?"

DAISY: "Ya, as long as I can remember. There's no jobs in Llano. After my mother died about a year later, he worked for the WPA [Works Progress Administration 1935-1943]. He rode a horse to Peñasco, and from there, I don't know where they work. He was in the WPA, him and another guy. I guess they went in a truck. But from Llano, they went to Peñasco, and they worked for the WPA for a long time, and then we moved to Colorado, and he start working there. I think for the WPA. I don't know."

NOTE: Eliu Quintana, brother of Manuel, was also a sheepherder in Wyoming. [Stanley]

Leaving New Mexico

RAYMOND: "When did you move there [Leadville]?"

DAISY: "After my mother died. Way after he got married, we were in Leadville. I think he had a little baby. It's a long time. I can't remember Raymond."

RAYMOND: "I remember Leadville. We all drove back there in a big red pickup."

DAISLY: "Ya, maybe that was the same red pickup. Oh, you mean."

RAYMOND: "He had that big red Ford pickup."

DAISY: "My dad?"

RAYMOND: "No, Casey had."

DAISY: "Oh, Ya."

RAYMOND: "We drove back to Leadville."

DAISY: "He made a camper. I think you were already six years old."

RAYMOND: "Living in the trailer court and all that kind of stuff."

Stringtown, Colorado

Stringtown, Colorado. Bucktown is the cluster of houses on the left. The Smelter is where the large buildings are. Grandpa Manuel lived across the road and up the hill from the smelter. My Mom and Dad, Mo and Nadine lived near the top left of the picture. Uncle Nelson and Uncle Ben lived next door. Our first cousin, Alfares Quintana, lived next to us. All of the area is dry and surrounded by round rocks and very few trees. [Picture from Google Earth Pro]

DAISY: "Ya, Dad in Bucktown, Colorado, downhill from Stringtown, and Nadine lived in Stringtown, Leadville. Horrible country. I remember it was gray there. Was by a factory [smelter] off to the side of the hill, and it was just belching smoke, and everything was just dirty."

Stanley, with casts on both feet in the arms of Uncle Tony. Tony is Aunt Daisy's brother. Uncle Tony became deaf as a young teenager when he fell off a "trastero" [dish cabinet]. Picture given to me by Aunt Daisy.

RAYMOND: "Stanley was kind of crippled up. Had braces on his legs or something."

DAISY: "He was a baby. Ya, he. I was in Leadville with your mother, and I went to Leadville to visit Nadine. That's when Stanley was born. He was born with his legs folded up."

RAYMOND: "So that was a birth defect?"

DAISY: "Ya, everything was twisted up inside the stomach, and they put braces when he was a tiny baby. And then, after that, I moved with your Mom. She told me there were a lot of jobs there. There wasn't. Well."

Nephew Stanley, age 2 in Stringtown. Note that the shoes don't have toes and were made to hold Stanley's feet turned out. Picture given to me by Aunt Daisy. About 1950.

NOTE: I was born with severely clubbed feet, had 3 surgeries, wore casts, and wore specially designed shoes to turn my toes outward for over a period of ten years. [Stanley]

Arl Raymond Kelso

RAYMOND: "She met my dad in Leadville. I guess."

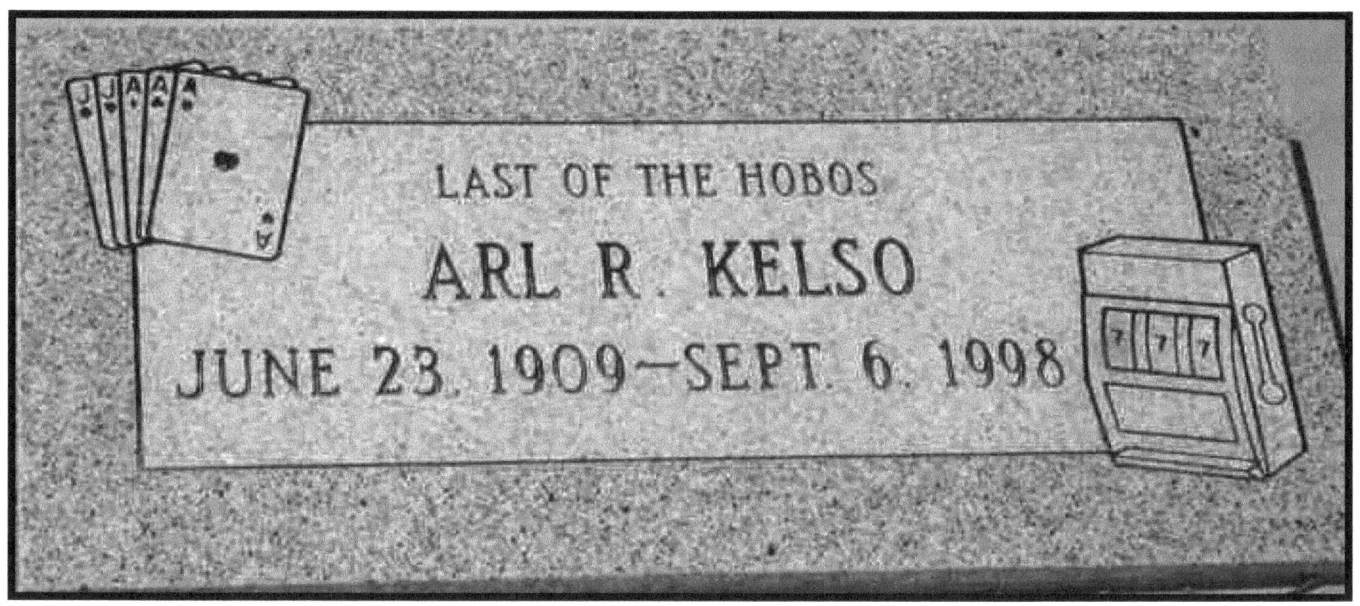

Brother in law Arl Raymond Kelso.

DAISY: "Ya, he was a barber. Cut hair there at the Windom [Vendome] hotel. That's where I worked making beds. They had a barbershop. Him and a black man were barbers. I don't know how he met her [Lucille]. She brought your dad to meet my dad, and my dad didn't want to meet him. [laughs] She just left with him to Denver. She just run off with him. My dad didn't want to meet him."

RAYMOND: "Okay, so she just took off?"

DAISY: "She just took off with him. Lucille, she'd do what she wanted. She didn't listen to my dad. She'd bring the boy to the house, and he didn't want to meet him. You know. Okay, so she left with him."

RAYMOND: "And I guess that's where my grandmother was probably living."

DAISY: "Ya, she took him to your grandmother's."

María Lucila "Lucille" Quintana Kelso Knight. Raymond's Mom. Lucille is Aunt Daisy's older sister. Picture given to me by Aunt Daisy.

RAYMOND: "Pearl [Raymond's grandmother]."

DAISY: "House, and they stay there for a long time."

RAYMOND: "In Aurora, I think."

DAISY: "In Aurora. In the meantime, we wrote to each other."

RAYMOND: "Ya."

DAISY: "Lucille and I, and they move from Aurora to Seattle. Where were you born, Seattle?"

RAYMOND: "Ya, I was born in Seattle."

DAISY: "That's when they moved to Seattle."

RAYMOND: "She said I was born in the county hospital, there, downtown or something."

DAISY: "She was making beds. She wrote me a letter saying she was making beds and she would carry you with her. You know, to work."

RAYMOND: "Ya."

California

DAISY: "And after that, she came home to Johannesburg. I don't think she came by herself. Maybe that's when she came to Leadville, when you were a baby. I don't know. She came from Seattle then."

RAYMOND: "So you saw. The first time. You saw me?"

DAISY: "You were about, I'd say 6 or 4 months. You were a tiny baby. You couldn't even crawl."

RAYMOND: "Then, ah, where did you see me?"

DAISY: "In Leadville, Colorado."

RAYMOND: "In Leadville?"

DAISY: "When she come in the train."

RAYMOND: "So she went from Aurora to Seattle?"

DAISY: "To Seattle to Aurora again, I guess. No to Johannesburg."

RAYMOND: "To Johannesburg, apparently because my grandmother was there. So apparently, that's when my grandmother moved. Was about that time."

DAISY: "Ya."

RAYMOND: "And I guess Arl [Raymond's dad] was off to Alaska or somewhere."

DAISY: "Ya. Arl was like my dad. He took off and left her alone. So she had you. So she probably wrote a letter to your Grandma 'cause she knew her."

RAYMOND: "Uh huh."

DAISY: "And probably your Grandma told her to come over there. Maybe that's how the story is. I don't know."

RAYMOND: "I don't think my grandmother wanted me."

DAISY: "Don't want you?"

RAYMOND: "Didn't want me over there. I don't."

DAISY: "She wanted you so much she spoiled you."

RAYMOND: "What? My grandmother?"

DAISY: "Ya. She used to put the shirts wrong side out so they won't pinch your delicate skin. I remember that."

RAYMOND: "She used to what?"

DAISY: [she laughs] "I said she use to have the shirts wrong side out. T-shirts."

RAYMOND: "Oh. The wrong side out?"

DAISY: "You know they got rough."

RAYMOND: "Oh. They weren't as rough, I guess."

DAISY: "Ya. They won't rub on your skin."

RAYMOND: "So I've been spoiled ever since. I guess."

DAISY: "She spoiled you. She liked you."

RAYMOND: "I kind of got the impression that she didn't really want my Mom and me around. At least that's what my Mom said."

DAISY: "Oh, your Mom! She didn't want your Mom, probably. She drank. Then you know. You never know."

RAYMOND: "Ya."

DAISY: "But she wanted you."

RAYMOND: "And then she probably went there, and then she went to visit you. I guess."

DAISY: "Who?"

RAYMOND: "My Mom with me."

DAISY: "No, no, that's the only time she went to visit me. When you was a tiny, tiny baby."

RAYMOND: "Ya. But I'm confused. Um, I was born in Seattle, and then you think my Mom and I went to Johannesburg?"

DAISY: "So the first time I seen you was when you was a tiny baby. The second is when I went to."

RAYMOND: "But you saw me in Leadville."

DAISY: "Okay."

RAYMOND: "And the next thing that happened is that you went to China Lake."

DAISY: "I went to China Lake to live with you guys."

RAYMOND: "Ya. Did you take the bus?"

DAISY: "Yes, and Lucille wrote me a letter how to get there. Said I have the permission. I had to have permission to go in there. In the base. She says Arl will make the permission for you to come in. So I come in on the bus. Led him up. Tell me, come in."

RAYMOND: "Okay."

DAISY: "I start walking. It was really blowing, and then I start walking."

RAYMOND: "That was at the front gate?"

DAISY:" Ya."

RAYMOND: "So you were let off at the front gate then?"

DAISY: "Ya, and then a jeep stop and told me you want a ride? And I said no. I want a taxi. They said we are the taxi. So I got in the jeep, and they took me to the prefabs."

RAYMOND: "So that's where we were living in the prefabs?"

DAISY: "Ya."

RAYMOND: "Okay."

DAISY: "And you were two and a half years old."

RAYMOND: "Two and a half?"

DAISY: "Ya."

RAYMOND: "Two and a half and living in the prefabs. Okay."

DAISY: "Two-bedroom house, but you sleep in the same room with them?"

DAISY: "Ya because. Um. So went to the prefabs. Prefabs and trailer."

RAYMOND: "How did we get to the trailer court?"

DAISY: "Well, that's, you know, I think we live there ten years because from the prefabs, I think they moved. You moved and went to Seattle again or someplace. You left the base. Your Mom and everybody and then you came back. Maybe a year later."

RAYMOND: "Huh. I wonder where we went."

DAISY: "I don't know where you went to. I don't know. Someplace. I thought you went to Seattle."

RAYMOND: "I don't know."

DAISY: "I don't know where you went."

RAYMOND: "And came back, and we ended up at the trailer court?"

DAISY: "Ya and your dad didn't have a barber. A barbers. He wasn't a barber anymore. He worked for the garbage."

RAYMOND: "The garbage folks?"

DAISY: "The garbage truck. Ya."

RAYMOND: "I certainly remember the old trailer park. I remember that."

DAISY: "That's when your dad went for the garbage department in the base. Okay. Oh, you know. I think he got laid off. Well, he worked at. I remember him as a barber at the big barbershop. Ya."

RAYMOND: "Um, down there. I remember that."

DAISY: "I don't know if he was laid off or he quit. But he was talking about leaving Lucille and all that."

RAYMOND: "Ya."

DAISY: "At that time, I not married and don't listen while I'm here 'cause I don't have a place to live. After I got married, we moved off base, and then that's when you guys moved."

RAYMOND: "So you got married and went off base?"

DAISY: "Ya, because we couldn't live on the base. Your Mom and Dad loaned us a trailer."

RAYMOND: "Oh, well. I thought Casey was working on the base."

DAISY: "He was working on the base, but we couldn't live on the base. You have to get on the list to get a house."

RAYMOND: "Oh. Ya. That's right. Okay."

DAISY: "We didn't have no trailer court, trailer, no nothing. Your dad had an old trailer. We live in it for a long time. The base has trailer courts."

RAYMOND: "Ya."

DAISY: "Got restrooms and everything. So we live in them. Little trailer, and we bought another one and live on the base for a long time. And then we moved to Lancaster."

RAYMOND: "Ya."

DAISY: "I didn't like Lancaster at all. I liked the base. The free buses and everything. [laughs] That's it. From there on, you know the story."

RAYMOND: "Well, kind of. So you took the bus?"

Nelson And Benito

RAYMOND: "Did, and I can't remember his name. Your blind brother."

Uncle Nelson was about age 18 before the mining accident that left him blind. Nelson was Aunt Daisy's brother. Picture given to me by Aunt Daisy.

DAISY: "Ya. Do you remember him?"

RAYMOND: "Ya. I remember him."

DAISY: "He lived next to Nadine."

NOTE: Uncle Nelson and Aunt Emilia Rodriguez lived next to us in Stringtown in the little house that Uncle Ben built. Uncle Nelson lost his vision in a mine explosion near Leadville when he was 18 years old. He was already married to Emilia. He told Emilia she was free to leave and not have to take care of a blind husband. She chose to stay. My Uncle Nelson played saxophone and drums with the Martinez Brothers. [Stanley]

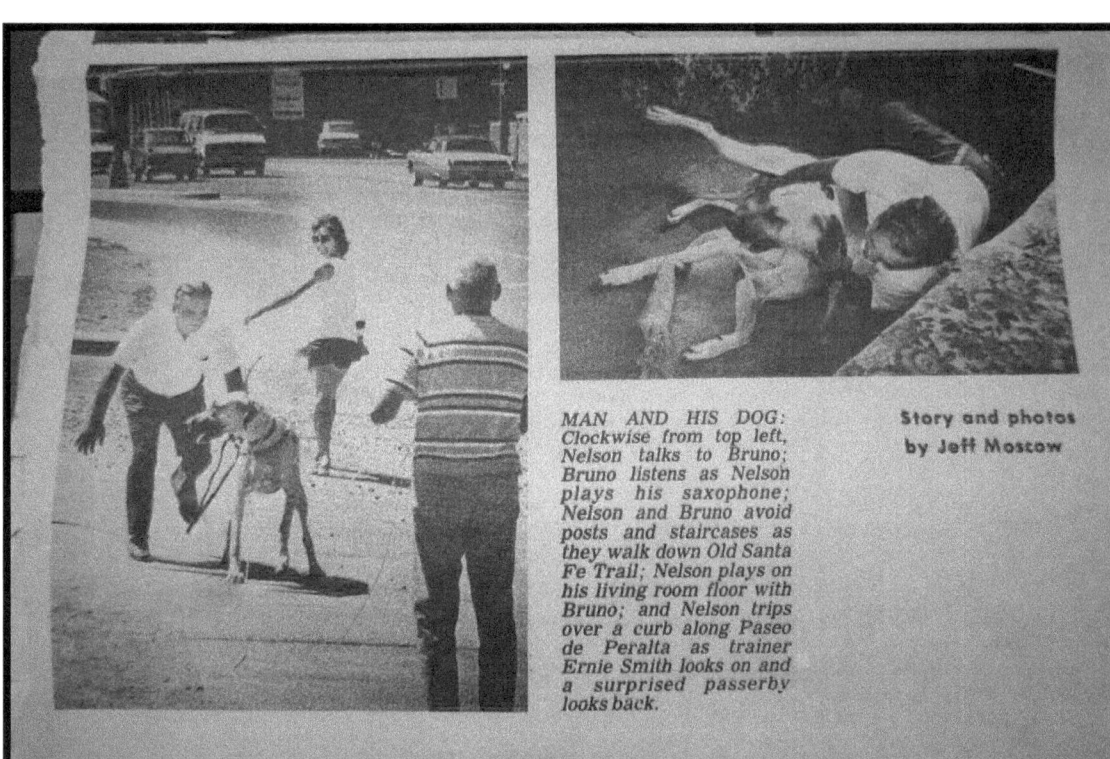

Uncle Nelson and his seeing eye dog in Santa Fe 1975. Uncle Nelson lived outside of the city limits, where there were dirt roads. Picture from La Vida, a newspaper in Santa Fe, New Mexico.

RAYMOND: "I remember something about them getting him a seeing-eye dog, and the seeing-eye dog didn't work because there wasn't any paved roads."

DAISY: "Ya, he lived in Santa Fe then."

RAYMOND: "There wasn't any paved roads and so."

DAISY: "Ya."

RAYMOND: "And he played music?"

DAISY: "Ya."

RAYMOND: "Ya. He played music but wasn't that some kind of mine accident or something?"

DAISY: "Smelter, he worked at the smelter."

RAYMOND: "Was that in Leadville?"

DAISY: "Leadville, Colorado."

RAYMOND: "Okay, and so there was an accident?"

DAISY: "He was 18 years old."

RAYMOND: "He was 18?"

DAISY: "He was only. He never knew George."

RAYMOND: "He never saw George? Okay."

DAISY: "He never saw George."

RAYMOND: "And that's his oldest son?"

DAISY: "I don't know if he was born when he got blind but I think he was born after he got blind."

RAYMOND: "Ya."

DAISY: "He never seen none of the kids. That's sad. At the time, I didn't think it was sad. But I think now it is sad."

RAYMOND: "Well, see. I don't remember him dying."

DAISY: "He died himself in New Mexico. I didn't go to the funeral. That was. We were living in Carson City then."

RAYMOND: "Oh, okay. I don't remember."

DAISY: " I know. It wasn't too long ago he died. After Benito died."

José Benito Quintana, brother of Aunt Daisy. Picture given to me by Aunt Daisy.

RAYMOND: "Oh, after Benito."

DAISY: "Ya, Benito died first."

RAYMOND: "Okay."

DAISY: "I was in. Don't know. Carson or Fernley. Maybe in Fernley. I don't know, but went to the funeral of Benito. And the one who let me know he died was Nelson. I got a phone call, and he said, "Benny is dead." He's the one that called me."

RAYMOND: "Ya and um. I remember my Mom not wanting to go at all. Didn't want to go back for anything to do with anything back there."

DAISY: "Ya, I know because."

RAYMOND: "Just a bunch of bad memories, I guess."

DAISY: "Yes, that's what's it. She had a hard time. She raised all those kids. Nobody came to see us. She raised Nelson. Nelson was living with us. Too many bad memories, and she didn't like that, I remember. I wanted to talk about Llano. She didn't want to hear about it. Too many bad memories for her. It was a hard life."

Lucille Danced And Drank

DAISY: "She had fun when she move out of there. She had fun when she went to China Lake. That's the reason she went wild. She never had fun in her life. [laughs] She'd dance and dance. Drank and dance."

RAYMOND: "Ya. That's a lot of fun, I think."

DAISY: "When she was growing up, we didn't go nowhere."

RAYMOND: "Well, I don't know what she saw in Jimmy [Lucille's husband]. I'll tell ya, man!"

DAISY: "I don't know either. I think because."

RAYMOND: "Oh, what a jerk."

DAISY: "I know. Well, Arl was a joke, too, but he didn't drink. Arl never touched a drop. Shaky [Daisy's husband] was the one who started the drinking. He took them on a picnic, and he gave them beer. Started drinking beer, but Arl never touched a drop. "

RAYMOND: "Ya."

DAISY: "Arl was nice with me. He was very polite, very nice. Jim was. Well, you see how we met Jim because your mother drank, so she associated with anybody that drank. If she wasn't drinking, she wouldn't married Jim. And he didn't want to get married. We went to Las Vegas, and I remember he was drunk, and she had to fill papers. Jim, he didn't want to, but he got married."

RAYMOND: "Well, I remember when you went."

DAISY: "Ya. You stayed."

RAYMOND: "I was in Lancaster."

DAISY: "Ya. "

RAYMOND: "You guys."

DAISY: "They asked the question "You been married before?" I said yes. She said no. What do you mean no? So I just stopped it. I didn't ask no more, and the woman that was signing the papers didn't make no difference to her. I don't know what she put, yes or no."

RAYMOND: "My mother. Arl told me that they were never married."

DAISY: "They wasn't, but I thought they was. When they asked that question, "You've been married before?" I said Ya. So, I thought automatically. [laughs] She told the lady no. That's when I knew she's not been married. So well, you see, I don't know. Probably the reason your Grandma didn't like her because she's an old lady. Old fashioned, you know."

RAYMOND: "Ya, she was old-fashioned."

DAISY: "You're supposed to be married in those days. No such thing as living together."

Casey [Shaky] and Daisy

María Daisy Quintana. Husband Ernest C. Shields, also know as "Casey" and "Shaky". Both pictures taken about 1948 and shared by Aunt Daisy's grandaughter, Desirae K.

RAYMOND: "Well, where did you and Casey get married?"

DAISY: "In Arkansas. "

RAYMOND: "Arkansas?"

DAISY: "We went to Kansas. We took the bus. Went to his mother, and we went to Arkansas and got married."

RAYMOND: "Who was in Arkansas, that you?"

DAISY: "Nobody. We just went there, just across the border. Maybe the license was cheaper. I don't know. Anyway, I made a mistake. I should have gotten married in California. I was dumb. I was dumb. I had to meet his father and mother. I was old-fashioned, too, you know. The difference. Got married there. Not waste the trip. I don't know. Everybody that I knew then, they're all dead anyway. Everyone is dead except Perry. All the Shields are almost dead. Ruthie's alive. Stay alive. Everybody's dead. All of them that were there. They're dead. We don't have to go there."

Jimmy And Lucille

RAYMOND: "Ya, I just remember all the tremendous fights that Jimmy and Mom would get into. Just knock down drag-out fights. Just."

DAISY: "They hit each other?"

RAYMOND: "Ya. Oh, Ya. One time, I remember livin' in the trailer court over there behind public works, where Jimmy took out all the food in the refrigerator and threw it outside the door. Just threw it all out."

DAISY: "Gee."

RAYMOND: "I called the cops on him probably three times."

DAISY: "You what?"

RAYMOND: "Called the cops. I had to run out, you know, and there was a phone where the bathrooms were. Ya. I called the cops."

DAISY: "They didn't take him to jail?"

RAYMOND: "No. They didn't take him to jail."

DAISY: "They didn't?"

RAYMOND: "They did not take him to jail."

DAISY: "That's funny after everything he did."

RAYMOND: "And, um, you know. They just fought. All the time. Fighting at the prefabs. Fighting in the trailer. Fighting all the time."

DAISY: "I don't know they fight like that."

RAYMOND: "Ya."

DAISY: "I knew they fought, but I didn't think it was that bad."

RAYMOND: "Oh, Ya. He would throw stuff. Throw beer cans. All kinds of stuff."

DAISY: "What?"

RAYMOND: "Beer cans. Um. He just went on and on and on."

DAISY: "You know when she stuck with him, she couldn't support herself."

RAYMOND: "Well, I think she egged him on a lot."

DAISY: "What? "

RAYMOND: "I think she egged him on a lot. Teased him to get him mad. I remember those kinds of things going on. I don't want to think about that stuff."

DAISY: "I know. That's like it was with Lucille."

RAYMOND: "I didn't want to think about that."

DAISY: "And finally he died, and he died a lonesome like, and so did Lucille."

RAYMOND: "Ya. I told Mom, "What [why] are you babysitting him? Let's put him in a home, and you can do whatever you want to do. You know there's plenty of money; you can do whatever you want to do."

DAISY: "And she didn't want to?"

RAYMOND: "I says said. She Lucille used to go to Las Vegas on the bus for a day."

DAISY: "By herself?"

RAYMOND: "On those party buses. You know. To Laughlin and all that, and I'm going. Why don't you go over there and stay awhile? Just get a room in any you can. I'll get you a room in any resort you want. You can stay there a week or a month. Whatever you want to do, Mom. Go have some fun."

David [Raymond's half-brother]

DAISY: "Ya, but you know there was David too."

RAYMOND: "This was. Ya. I mean, David could. Ah."

DAISY: "After David was dead?"

RAYMOND: "Ya."

DAISY: "I don't know."

RAYMOND: "David got real weird on me too."

DAISY: "What do you mean?"

RAYMOND: "Well. I mean he was going to church and just. Ah. He was restricting Mom's money. He would only give her $300 a month."

DAISY: "Ya. I know that."

RAYMOND: "What are you saving it for? What are you saving all this stuff for? You guys can buy anything you want. Redecorate the house. Get whatever you want, and I should of. I should never had David take care of the finances. He got guardianship through the court."

DAISY: "Yes."

RAYMOND: "I'm buying my daughter a used car."

DAISY: "Oh, okay."

RAYMOND: "You know she's going to school and doing the best she can, and so I'm paying her rent and so on."

DAISY: "What daughter is that? The young one?"

RAYMOND: "Sierra. She's trying real hard to get a degree. Real hard. She's always had a problem in school. But I mean, there was all this money all the time that my mother could do anything she wants. "Mom. Do you want to move out of this house? You know David died here. Want to get away from here?" "No. It's nice and close to the store and all this stuff. And I says, "What do you want? I'll just get it. Do you want a bigger TV?"

DAISY: "I offer her to come over and stay with me a month. She didn't want to."

RAYMOND: "Ya. She didn't want to do anything."

DAISY: "I know. She just want the bottle."

RAYMOND: "And I know Daisy. I could not ever find her drinking."

DAISY: "I know she drank secretly."

RAYMOND: "And I don't think she ever drank that much. I don't think she was a drinker. A six-pack a day or anything like that."

Diabetes

RAYMOND: "I think it's the diabetes thing. It's there, and I don't think it took one beer. Really, just knock her flat."

DAISY: "That's what it was, and so that's just like Tony."

RAYMOND: "And the diabetes thing which we all have. You know? I have a touch of."

DAISY: "You do?"

RAYMOND: "A little bit. I'm taking stuff for diabetes."

DAISY: "What do you mean, a little bit?"

RAYMOND: "Well, I'm on the border."

DAISY: "Oh."

RAYMOND: "I don't have to watch my diet if I don't want to, basically."

DAISY: "See, all my kids have diabetes. I don't. Clarence is."

RAYMOND: "Well, Clarence said he had a touch of it. So."

DAISY: "I don't know if I have it or not. I can't take my blood. I'm scared to punch my finger."

RAYMOND: "Ya, I get it. I go. I've got high blood pressure and high cholesterol and all those old diseases."

DAISY: "I do too. I don't know if I got high blood pressure, but you know everybody's sickly nowadays. On my days, they die young, too. Anyway, they didn't know what's the matter, anyway."

DAISY: "Your mother had liver problems and diabetes. She drank one beer, she got drunk. But I could never drink. We used to go to Carson City to another bar. Shaky didn't want her in his bar, and they would pile the beer in front of us. I have five or six beers in front of me. I told them I don't want no more, no more, no more. I could only drink one. I can't drink much."

RAYMOND: "Well, you're too small."

DAISY: "No. When I drink one beer, it's really good, and the second beer pain gets in my stomach and never goes away. I've got pancreatitis. You know what pancreatitis is?"

RAYMOND: "No."

DAISY: "Well, when I was in San José, everything made me sick. So, I went for tests at Kaiser for six months. They put a tube in my mouth. Into my pancreas, I guess."

RAYMOND: "That's right. I remember now."

DAISY: "And then they pulled it out, and they said I couldn't digest fat. I have inflamed pancreas, and I take Vicodin every time I eat, and I feel good. I think Vicodin is enzyme."

RAYMOND: "Ya."

DAISY: "What you call that word?"

RAYMOND: "Enzymes. Ya."

DAISY: "I'm great now."

RAYMOND: "What about Patti? Does Patti have anything like that?"

DAISY: "She has diabetes."

RAYMOND: "Ya. Well, okay."

DAISY: "Diabetes."

RAYMOND: "Okay."

DAISY: "It's inherent, and Casey got diabetes."

RAYMOND: "Ya. Got it, too."

DAISY: "You don't have it very bad, though, because he takes many pills."

RAYMOND: "I'm taking too many pills too."

DAISY: "Medical pills?"

RAYMOND: "Ya. Ya. Two different pills for high blood pressure. One for diabetes. Apirin to thin the blood. I got something else I'm taking. I can't even remember what it's for."

DAISY: "Two pills for high blood pressure. You must have it very high."

RAYMOND: "What high blood pressure? Ya."

DAISY: "I got one. I take one."

RAYMOND: "The, um, I think it's a lot better now since I retired."

DAISY: "Oh, Ya."

RAYMOND: "And I'll wean myself off that here, hopefully."

DAISY: "Ya. It depends on how you live. You know, high blood pressure. You get mad or worried, get depressed; Blood pressure is fun. Very funny and you have to be in control of your life and be calm. Who can live calm in this world? You know?"

RAYMOND: "You certainly don't want to watch the news or anything like that. That's just silly."

DAISY: "I don't want to preach to you, but that's what the Bible says. We're living the last days, and it's not going to get better. You can see it's not going to get any better. Sons are killing their fathers. Sons are killing the sons. It never happened before. I want to have fun. I want to go dance. [laughter] That's the way when Lucille and me were young. All we did. She came over with Jim, and you, and Shaky to see Clarence in Elko. Remember, and we put on the radio or tape. I don't know what, and we started dancing. Me and her in the trailer, and Jim would laugh and clap the hands after we got through. We were just simple. Simple things we did. We did go out and being [did] nothing. Well, that's Shaky. Interfere with young people. We don't interfere with us here. He thought he'd interfere with you and Clarence. Young folks. Shaky was old. They sure let him interfere with them. He interferes with us. Well anyway, that's it."

RAYMOND: "Ya. Better call it a day."

Back To Life In Llano

DAISY: "We ate. We always had beans and potatoes and, of course, tortillas. We couldn't cook bread."

RAYMOND: "I'm getting hungry right now."

DAISY: "I can't eat tortillas. I like them. There's another thing. I'm allergic to gluten. So I had these attacks at home when I was little. I remember that my mother used to call "perjo." I don't know what "perjos" is in English. "Perjos" [is] in Spanish. I had attacks on my digestion, you know. That's when I went to the doctor, they thought I had gluca. Allergic to gluten. Probably still now because I love tortillas. But when I eat a lot, I got the same attack."

RAYMOND: "Ya."

DAISY: "I pass out mucus in my bowels."

RAYMOND: "Probably your pancreas was talking to you then."

DAISY: "Ya. I don't eat too much of that stuff anymore. I eat a little bread but mostly potatoes. Potatoes are good. Potatoes, corn, corn tortillas. Yes. At home, I had those attacks, so I had those all my life. Well, anyway, I'll let you go."

RAYMOND: "Ya. We better jump off the phone."

Nadine

DAISY: "Really good since she was little, but I think since she grown up. Her kids turned her against me."

RAYMOND: "I thought she turned her kids against us. I guess. I called Stanley. I just thought for sure he was gonna come to my mother's funeral, and I wanted him to play guitar. I asked him if he would do that, and he said, "I can't." I kinda thought that if it was up to him, he would of come. But since it was, you know, his mother kind of interfered with that decision."

NOTE: I remember being invited to Aunt Lucille's funeral, but we didn't have enough money for me to go, and I couldn't afford to take time off of work. [Stanley]

DAISY: "I don't know."

RAYMOND: "I didn't talk."

DAISY: "How is Brook? She is the evil one. She wrote a letter. Did you see that?"

RAYMOND: "The."

DAISY: "She's the one who turn us in against everybody. She is against Noel. You know. What you read about him."

RAYMOND: "Well."

DAISY: "Because Mo wasn't his father, that's why. Stupid like they knew that."

NOTE: Noel Dean Lucero is listed as the son of Mom and Dad on his birth certificate, baptism certificate, marriage record, and death certificate. Noel is the son of Juan Amadeo 'Mo' Lucero and María Lourdes 'Nadine' Quintana. The only way to prove he "might" not be the son of Mo is through a DNA test, but we don't have a sample of his DNA. I don't know who Brook is. [Stanley]

RAYMOND: "Okay."

DAISY: "Understand what I'm saying, they treated Noel like an outcast. Bert, not Stanley. Bert."

About 1959 in Sringtown. Stanley, Noel, and Bert. Nephews of Daisy. Picture given to me by my Mom.

RAYMOND: "Bert is the middle child, right? It's Stanley, Bert, and Noel?"

Noel and Nadine a few months before Noel died. Nadine's son, Noel, is Aunt Daisy's nephew. Picture taken by Stanley Lucero.

DAISY: "Ya. But Nadine was very close to Noel. I thought she'd go nuts when he died. I thought she was really going to get depressed, but she sounded real good."

RAYMOND: "She sounded real good. She sounded real good and."

DAISY: "Wanda said she didn't look good. "

NOTE: Wanda is the oldest daughter of my Uncle Ben. She is my Aunt Daisy's niece. She talked to Aunt Daisy on the phone after Noel died. Noel lived with Mom for many years. He was closer to Mom than Bert and I. Mom, Nadine, had advanced diabetes. She had dialysis for several years and was totally bedridden the last year of her life. She finally asked to be taken off of dialysis, placed on hospice, and died ten days later. Maríano and I were driving to Albuquerque when Bert called to say Mom died. [Stanley]

RAYMOND: "Well, I don't know."

DAISY: "He was a diabetic. Noel was, and his girlfriend was giving him insulin."

RAYMOND: "Well, you know Stanley and I talked about that a little bit ago. "

NOTE: I have been on insulin for many years but am still in good to fair health. [Stanley]

Other Health Issues

RAYMOND: "He had diabetes, and I've got a touch of it. You know we all do."

DAISY: "You got diabetes, too?"

RAYMOND: "Me? Yes."

DAISY: "Well, everybody."

RAYMOND: "Ya. Everybody got it."

DAISY: "It's an epidemic."

RAYMOND: "Well, it's hereditary."

NOTE: Grandpa Manuel died of complications of diabetes. [Stanley]

DAISY: "Well, everybody in Fernley got diabetes."

RAYMOND: "You know, it's hereditary, and I think the other thing is that people are living longer now, and so, you just get it. It comes with the old age. You know? It comes with old age."

DAISY: "But haven't seen Noel yet, huh? In the coffin or nothing?"

RAYMOND: "I don't think so, and Stanley hasn't shown yet."

DAISY: "Who?"

RAYMOND: "Stanley."

DAISY: "He's leaving today. He left today."

RAYMOND: "Oh, I thought he was going to arrive. He's leaving at 5."

Note By Raymond

The following is on the last few minutes of the tape. Most of which were discussions with Clarence about Nadine at Tony's funeral. Daisy speaking of experiences with Nadine wanting Tony to buy their Dad's property. Nadine trying to borrow Tony's car. Nadine saying that she doesn't have a sister named Daisy; that Nadine believes that Lucille and Daisy gave her away, which is not true. Ray speaking of missing Barbara and how angry she is. The only part of this section that was pertinent to the family history was after I asked a question for Stanley.

María Dolores Quintana and daughter María Rumalda Quintana. Rumalda is Aunt Daisy's grandmother. Dolores is Aunt Daisy's great-grandmother. Picture given to my Mom by Armando Martínez, neighbor of Dolores in Peñasco, New Mexico. The picture was probably taken before 1920 by a professional photographer.

RAYMOND: "What can you remember about your grandmother and grandfather, their physical look?"

DAISY: "Grandmother [Rumalda] tall on my mother's side. I remember her walking like a deer from Peñasco to Llano every two weeks. Grandfather [Esteban] was half-brother of Rumalda. They were brother and sister. My Mom [Lupita] and Dad [Manuel] are first cousins. Grandfather [Esteban] tall and light-skinned. Grandmother [Librada] on father's side looked like an Indian. She sang in Indian to me. She could sing in Spanish and Indian. This grandmother was short. Looked like an Indian. She had bangs like Indian women. Other grandmother [Rumalda] was tall. I have a picture; don't you have a picture?"

NOTE BY STANLEY:

Several relatives have asked me if we are affiliated with any Native American Tribe. The answer is NO. We are a mix of several Native American tribes, but I have not found any of our ancestors listed on any tribal rolls. My maternal Family Tree DNA is mtDNA Haplogroup A2h1. My maternal line is: María Lourdes Quintana > María Guadalupe Martínez . María Rumalda Quintana > María Dolores Quintana. "Haplogroup A is found in eastern Eurasia and throughout the Americas. This haplogroup was present in the populations that initially colonized the pre-Columbian Americas and dates to at least 30,000 years ago." (Quote from my FamilyTree DNA Account Kit #81329).

RAYMOND: "Two older women, one tall. Both."

DAISY: "Mother and daughter [Dolores and Rumalda]. Grandmother tall, great grandmother short, Dolores. Think she was more Indian than anyone else."

RAYMOND: "Nadine says it's Apache."

DAISY: "Indians in Peñasco are Navajo."

RAYMOND: "I think more Pueblo than Navajo."

This Concludes The Interviews Of Aunt Daisy.
Comments By Raymond

Interviews with Aunt Daisy in Fernley, Nevada. Saturday, August 17, 2011. This portion of the book consists of comments by Raymond.

"My Mom, Lucille, was 15. My Aunt Daisy was 14. My Grandpa Manuel had a job with the WPA [Works Progress Administration 1941].

Grandpa became a sheepherder in Wyoming for 6 months at a time. Manuel had credit at the local market while he was gone. My mother [Lucille] was the oldest and took care of the rest of the kids. She quit school. There was no electricity, water from the ditch, and a wood burning stove.

My grandmother died in childbirth. The baby was dead and Lupe was very, very sick. There were only 2 cars in Llano. My mother got the schoolteacher to take her mother to the hospital in Taos where she died 4 days later with my mother by her side. Meanwhile, the dead baby Franklin was in the cellar. Lupe was brought back to the house for the wake and laid on the table. Tony was two and a half years old and kept asking, "When is my Mom going to wake up?" The baby was buried with my grandmother in Llano. Manuel did not make it to the funeral as he was still in Wyoming.

Later, Manuel came home in a pickup and took everyone to Colorado to pick potatoes and peas. When my mother was about 19, her father Manuel came home with a girlfriend younger than my mother from Peñasco. My mother was very upset and ran off with her brother Nelson and maybe went back to Llano. The family then moved to Leadville, Colorado. Manuel worked in the smelter. My mother worked as a dishwasher in the only hotel in Leadville and met my father, a barber, in the same hotel.

My mother did not want to leave her younger brothers and sisters but went to Aurora, Colorado. They Mom and Dad then went to Seatle, where I was born. My father then took off to Alaska for a barber job. This upset my mother and she left Seattle and visited Daisy in Leadville on her way to Johannesburg to stay with my father's mother, Pearl Kelso (my grandmother, a school teacher). This upset my grandmother, who told my father to come home from Alaska. My mother and father were never married.

Sometime later, Daisy came to Ridgecrest to live with my mother. They both cleaned houses and babysat. Daisy met Casey.

Clarence was born in 1950. I remember Daisy in the hospital in Trona the day Clarence was born. I was 5 years old.

My Aunt Daisy is very proud of Lucille. She said that my mother raised her and her brothers and sisters for 5 years. She was Daisy's best friend, mother, and sister. She had a very hard life. She learned good behavior very young. She did not let men in the house. No church. She babied me, and I was very spoiled."

Dad Manuel, Mom Lupita, Aunt Altagracia and Uncle Ezquiel. Altagracia and Ezequiel lived in Salt Lake City. Picture given to me by Aunt Daisy.

María Daisy Quintana

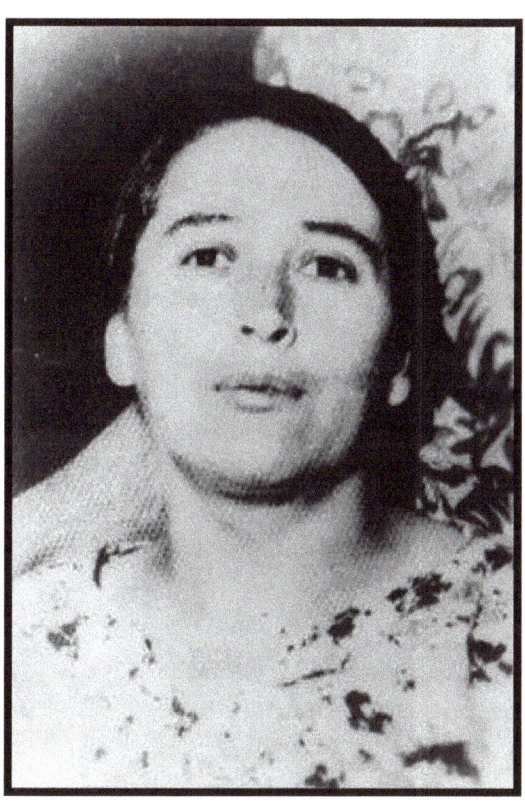

Altagracia Quintana Martínez. Aunt Daisy's aunt. Altagracia is the daughter of José Remijio Martínez and María Rumalda Quintana. Altagracia married Ezequiel Leiba. She died and was buried in Salt Lake City. Picture from Find A Grave.

María Antonia Quintana. Aunt Daisy's grand aunt. Half sister of Juan Esteban and Rumalda Quintana. Married to Francisco Roibal. Picture shared by María Armijo Rodríguez.

L-R Steve, Augustin, Lee, Leroy, Isidor, and George in Colorado Springs at Uncle Tony's funeral. Aunt Daisy's step-brothers [Steve, Agustin, Leroy, and Isidor] and nephews [Lee and George]. Picture shared by Jackie Quintana from Española, New Mexico. Picture taken in 2003.

Ancestors Of María Daisy Quintana

Google Map Of The Peñasco Valley, New Mexico.

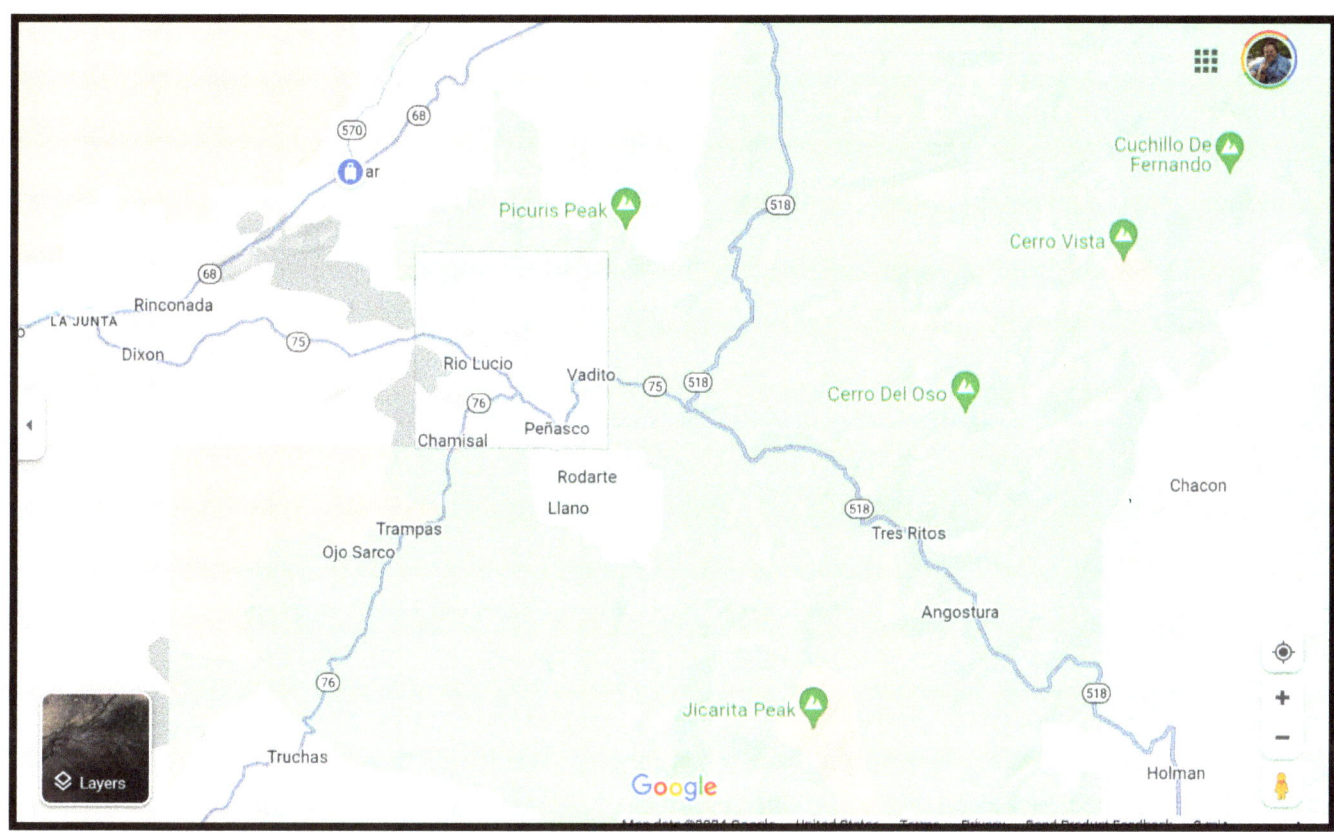

Our ancestors have lived near each other in the Peñasco Valley in southern Taos County, New Mexico, USA, for hundreds of years. They lived in Llano, Trampas, Chamisal, Rodarte, Peñasco, Rio Lucio, and Chamisal.

Records For María Daisy Quintana

October 14, 1923. San Antonio Catholic Church. Daisy María Quintana from Llano de San Juan. Born 14 Oct 1923. Baptized 27 Oct 1923 in Peñasco. Daughter of Manuel Quintana & Lupita Martínez. Nomina Patrinorum: B Vigil & Rafaelita Vigil.

April 9, 1930. US Federal Census, New Mexico, Taos County, Llano, Precinct 8. Quintana, Daisy, daughter, lives on a farm, female, white, age 5, single, never attended school, born in New Mexico, father born in New Mexico, mother born in New Mexico. Living with Manuel [head, age 27], Lupita [wife, age 28], Lusila [daughter, age 7], Nelson [son, age 3], and Bessy [daughter, age 11/12].

April 22, 1940, US Federal Census, New Mexico, Taos County, Precinct #8. Quintana, Daisy, granddaughter, female, white, age 13, single, born in New Mexico. Living with Juan E [head, age 73], Librita [wife, age 70], and Elvie [son, age 27].

December 21, 1948. Arkansas County. Marriage Index 1837-1957. María Daisy Quintana, female, age 24, born about 1924, residence China Lake, Kern, California. Spouse Ernest C Shields, male, age 24. Marriage County Benton.

April 25, 1950. US Federal Census. California, Kern County, Township 14 (N.O.T.S), Trailer Court. Shields, Daisy M, wife, white female, age 26, married, born in New Mexico, works at home, not looking for work. Living with Shields, Ernest C [head age 28, munitions worker Naval Ordinance].

April 4, 2015, U.S. Veterans Gravesite, ca. 1775-2019. Daisy Marie Shields. Rank SN 2/C. Death age 91. Birthdate 18 Oct 1923. Death date 4 Apr 2015. Internment place Pernley, Nevada, USA. Cemetery. Address: 14 Veterans Way. Cemetery postal code 89408. Cemetery Northern Nevada Veterans Memorial Cemetery, Section 0a, Plot 589, World War II, US Navy. Relative Ernest Clay Shields. Comments wife.

THE END

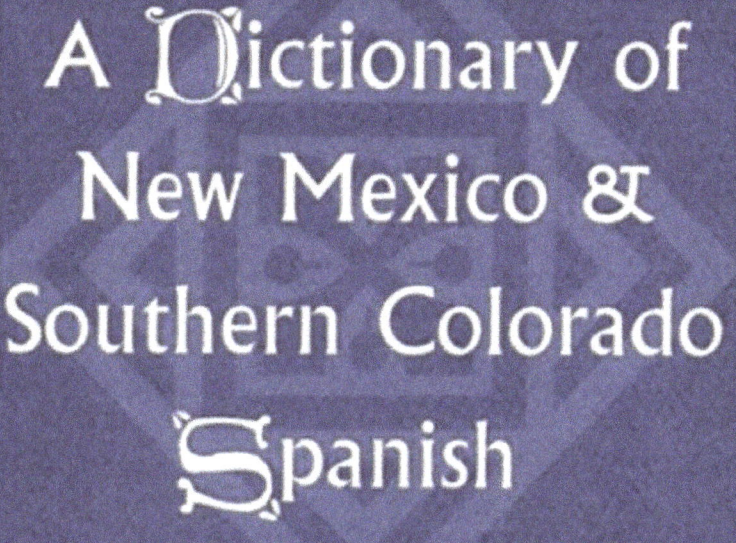

Author's Note:

I hope you enjoyed reading Aunt Daisy's comments as much as I did. I learned so much about life in Llano after the loss of the common lands and what our family had to do to survive. My Aunts, Uncles, and cousins currently live in New Mexico, Colorado, Montana, Wyoming, Virginia, Utah, and California.

I found that I could almost hear the voices of my relatives while reading the transcripts.

Aunt Daisy and Raymond are speaking a dialect of English unique to northern New Mexico.

For more information about our unique Spanish language, refer to the dictionary of new mexico & southern colorado spanish by Ruben Cobos.

Thank you for sharing your pictures.

Alberto Vidaurre

Armando Martínez

Dallas Quintana Eggelmeyer

Desirae K [Aunt Daisy's granddaughter]

Genoveva Lucero Martínez

Jackie Quintana

María Armijo Rodríguez

María Daisy Quintana "Aunt Daisy

María Lourdes "Nadine" Quintana

Raymond Kelso

Yolanda María Lucero

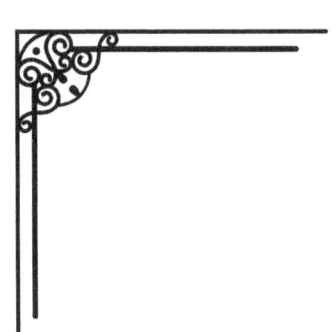 

Thank You For Contributing Your Time And Efforts To Prepare This Book For Publicaton.

Nora Guillen

Raymond Kelso

Yolanda M Lucero

 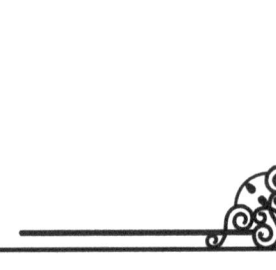

www.ingramcontent.com/pod-product-compliance
Lightning Source LLC
Chambersburg PA
CBHW061353010526

44107CB00011B/924